Explode The Code®

Essential lessons for phonics mastery

3

Nancy Hall • Rena Price

Mad

Made

EDUCATORS PUBLISHING SERVICE

Cambridge and Toronto

Cover: Hugh Price
Text illustrations: Laura Price and Alan Price

Printed in Mayfield, PA, in April 2013
ISBN 978-0-8388-1462-8

22 23 24 25 26 PAH 17 16 15 14 13

a, e, i, o, u, and sometimes *y* are vowels.

◯ the vowels.

bat	it
rib	fed
club	bank
on	fat
tub	skunk
slap	box

a, e, i, o, u, and sometimes y are vowels. Sometimes vowels say their names.

◯ the vowel that says its name.

ⓔ i o	i e o
a o u	i u a
a i o	u o e
o a e	e u o

In each word below, the vowel says its name.

◯ the vowels.

g**o**	I
we	he
hi	so
no	be

**If a vowel is at the end of a little word,
the vowel says its name.**

(⬭) it.

(me) or men?	he or hen?
we or wet?	yes or yo-yo?
hill or hi?	no or net?
go or got?	hop or ho-ho?

Read, write, and X it.

he			
_h_ _e_			
we			
_ _			
go			
_ _			
me			
_ _			
yo-yo			
_ _ - _ _			
hi			
_ _			
no			
_ _			

If a little word ends in y, the y says /ī/.

$\bigcirc$ it.

drop or (dry)?	trap or try?
crib or cry?	mitt or my?
flat or fly?	sky or skin?
spy or spin?	Fred or fry?

Read, write, and X it.

my __ __			
cry __ __ __			
fry __ __ __			
sky __ __ __			
spy __ __ __			
dry __ __ __			
fly __ __ __			

Match and write it.

| sky | fry | ~~we~~ | yo-yo | no |
| me | go | cry | spy | fly |

_we_

8

Yes or no?

	No	Yes
Can a sled fly in the sky?	☒	☐
Can he fry an egg in a pan?	☐	☐
Will Sam cry if he is sad?	☐	☐
Will we trap a bad spy?	☐	☐
Can a cat swim in the sky?	☐	☐
Will a rug try to go to bed?	☐	☐
Is a wet duck dry?	☐	☐

Write it.

cry

Put a silent e at the end of a word, and the vowel before it says its name.

Add a silent e to the words below. Does your word fit the picture?

c u t   ⎯⎯⎯⎯⎯⎯⟶   _c_ _u_ _t_ _e_

m a d   ⎯⎯⎯⎯⎯⎯⟶   _ _ _ _

c u b   ⎯⎯⎯⎯⎯⎯⟶   _ _ _ _

T i m   ⎯⎯⎯⎯⎯⎯⟶   _ _ _ _

c a p   ⎯⎯⎯⎯⎯⎯⟶   _ _ _ _

If a word has silent e at the end, the vowel says its name.

◯ the vowel that says its name, and X the silent e.

c(u)t**e**✗	made
home	here
line	cube
gate	pine
tube	pole

Read, write, and X it.

cane			
_ _ _ _			
cute			
_ _ _ _			
cape			
_ _ _ _			
cube			
_ _ _ _			
pine			
_ _ _ _			
made			
_ _ _ _			
time			
_ _ _ _			

13

5/22

cap or **cape?**	pin or **pine?**
mad or **made?**	cub or **cube?**
can or **cane?**	cut or **cute?**
cut or cute	cube or **cub?**
cap or **cape?**	mad or **made?**

Match and write it.

5/22

cane ~~cane~~   cape   cub   ~~cap~~   can

made   kite   time   cube   cute

cute

made

cape

time

can

cub

kite

cube

Spell.   Write.

	(k) t	(i) e	(te) t	**kite**
	s c	i a	p pe	
	b c	u o	te t	
	n m	i a	d de	
	g c	a o	n ne	
	t p	u i	ne n	
	b c	u o	be b	

16

Yes or no?

	No	Yes
Will a cape cry?	☐	☐
Can you put a cub in a glass?	☐	☐
Will a cat make its bed?	☐	☐
Do you fly a kite?	☐	☐
Will a crab use a cane?	☐	☐
Is a pine made of brass?	☐	☐
Is it time to go to bed?	☐	☐

X it.

Sam has a cane and a cape.	☐	
Sam has a cap in a can.	☐	
Pat made a red kite.	☐	
Pat is made at the cute cat.	☐	
Jim has the same pet as Jan.	☐	
Jim has the same pot as Jan.	☐	
Ann has a cube in the glass.	☐	
Ann has a cub in the glass.	☐	
Tim will fly in the sky.	☐	
Time can go by fast.	☐	
The cute duck will try to swim.	☐	
The duck will try to cut the bun.	☐	
The big clock has no hands.	☐	
Tim tells the clock his plan.	☐	

18

Write it.

19

⬭ it. tub tube tab	Sam Same Sand
robe rob rode	tub tap tube
rob robe rode	ham hog home
rat rake rate	rod rope rode
pill pole pile	coke cat cake

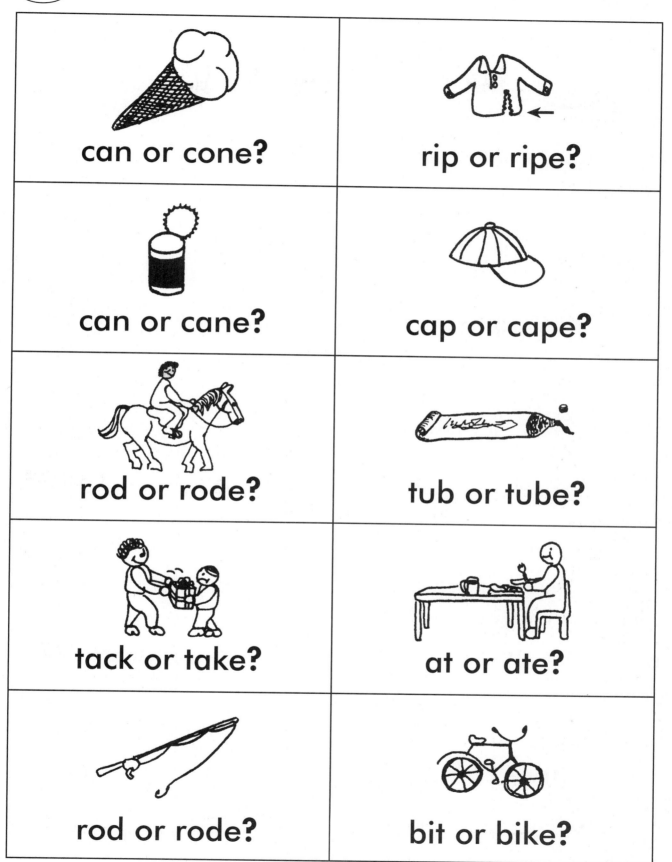

can or cone?

rip or ripe?

can or cane?

cap or cape?

rod or rode?

tub or tube?

tack or take?

at or ate?

rod or rode?

bit or bike?

Read, write, and X it.

bike _ _ _ _			
tube _ _ _ _			
rod _ _ _			
cake _ _ _ _			
game _ _ _ _			
lake _ _ _ _			
home _ _ _ _			

22

Match and write it.

home   lake   tube   rope   cone

cake   take   rake   ate   same

_____

_____

_____

_____

_____

_____

_____

_____

	Spell.			Write.
	t c	a u	ck ke	_____
	t c	u o	be b	_____
	b p	i a	ke te	_____
	c r	a u	ck ke	_____
	t p	u i	be b	_____
	n r	a o	d pe	_____
	c s	o i	me ne	_____

Yes or no?

	No	Yes
Can you swim in a lake?	☐	☐
Can a plum be ripe?	☐	☐
Will a cake fly in the sky?	☐	☐
Is it fun to ride a bike?	☐	☐
Will a doll lick a cone?	☐	☐
Can a kite fit in a pipe?	☐	☐
Can you rope a fly?	☐	☐

X it.

We will swim in the lake. ☐

We will sled on the lake. ☐

Sal rode in a pine tub. ☐

Sal rode on a fat tube. ☐

The twins ate the same cake. ☐

The twins ate the same cape. ☐

Brad grabs the cone. ☐

The frog licks the cone. ☐

Tom will rake a big pile. ☐

Tom will take a fat pill. ☐

Jane gave a cake to Dad. ☐

Dad gave a pet to Jane. ☐

Fred rode home in his truck. ☐

A fox rode home on Fred's bike. ☐

Write it.

27

⬭ it. ➜	flame flap flip
	mile smile stile
	stop stove stone
	slide smell snarl
	plant plate plane
	smoke smock snore
	drip drive dive
	stone stack stove
	flap flake lake
	broke bride blade

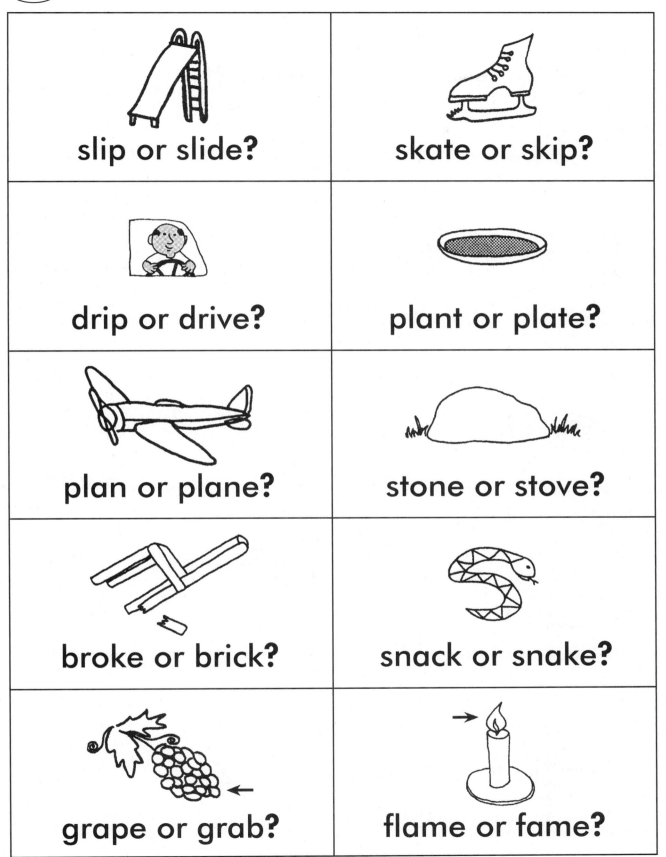

slip or slide?

skate or skip?

drip or drive?

plant or plate?

plan or plane?

stone or stove?

broke or brick?

snack or snake?

grape or grab?

flame or fame?

Read, write, and X it.

plate			
_ _ _ _ _			
stone			
_ _ _ _ _			
stove			
_ _ _ _ _			
smoke			
_ _ _ _ _			
plane			
_ _ _ _ _			
broke			
_ _ _ _ _			
skate			
_ _ _ _ _			

Match and write it.

smile	drive	snake	grape	plane
slide	stove	skate	broke	stone

	sm st	o a	ne n	
	sl st	o i	ck de	
	sp sn	o a	ke ne	
	sm sk	a o	te ke	
	st sn	i a	ck ke	
	sm sl	a i	le me	
	st sm	o e	v ve	

Yes or no?

	No	Yes
Can you slip on a slide?	☐	☐
Will Tom smile if he is sad?	☐	☐
Can Jane drive home?	☐	☐
Can you skate on a plate?	☐	☐
Will you get a snake as a snack?	☐	☐
Can you make smoke with a fire?	☐	☐
Can a cat slide into home plate?	☐	☐

X it.

Steve will not smile. ☐
Steve will not smell. ☐

Kate can fly a plane. ☐
Kate drove up the steps. ☐

Fred skates in the game. ☐
Fred skips by the gate. ☐

The plate broke on the stove. ☐
The pipe broke the stone. ☐

The plate will fly in the sky. ☐
The cute fly has a plane. ☐

The snake smiles at Dave. ☐
Dave smells the snack. ☐

The snake slid on the steps. ☐
The slide has a sock on it. ☐

Write it.

sh says /sh/ as in <u>sh</u>ell.

X the picture that begins with /sh/.

sh-			
sh-			
sh-			

Listen for /sh/ at the end as in fi<u>sh</u>.

X the picture that ends with /sh/.

-sh			
-sh			
-sh			

it.

shot / shop / **ship**	**ship** / shell / sell
dash / **brush** / dish	crust / crash / **crush**
hut / **shut** / shop	share / save / **shave**
cash / **crash** / crust	**shed** / shot / sled
rust / rash / **rush**	track / **trash** / truck

37

Read, write, and X it.

shade ____			
shop ____			
shell ____			
ship ____			
fish ____			
dish ____			
shine ____			

38

Match and write it.

dish	ship	brush	shed	shave
crash	shell	shop	shade	shine

_____

_____

_____

_____

_____

_____

_____

_____

Spell.   Write.

	st sh	e a	lt ll
	f g	a i	m sh
	st sh	a o	p d
	sn sh	e u	d t
	sh sl	a o	pe ve
	gr br	o u	st sh
	cr c	i a	sh ss

Yes or no?

	No	Yes
Is a ship big?	☐	☐
Will a shell trot?	☐	☐
Can a dish shave?	☐	☐
Can I brush a pet?	☐	☐
Can a ship grin?	☐	☐
Will a fish swim well?	☐	☐
Can a sled crash on a hill?	☐	☐

X it.

The shell is big.	☐	
The shed is big.	☐	
A cute fish is in the dish.	☐	
A cute fish is on the ship.	☐	
The lake will shine in the sun.	☐	
Jane will stand in the shade.	☐	
Jeff will try to brush the fish.	☐	
Jeff will dry the brush in the sun.	☐	
The flat plate can crack if it drops.	☐	
The fat plane will crash if it flips.	☐	
My brush has a smile.	☐	
My brush has a smell.	☐	
Dave drove his bike in the sand.	☐	
Dave rode his bike in the trash.	☐	

Write it.

th says /th/ as in <u>th</u>umb.

X the picture that begins with /th/.

th-			

th-			

th-			

wh says /wh/ as in <u>wh</u>eel.

X the picture that begins with /wh/.

wh-			

wh-			

wh-			

44

throne tone trot	bat bath path
bath path pats	bath brat bat
think trick tick	whip which hick
white wit while	whale wham when
truck trash trip	thin think thick

45

Read, write, and X it.

them			
_ _ _ _			
think			
_ _ _ _ _			
thin			
_ _ _ _			
math			
_ _ _ _			
wham			
_ _ _ _			
whine			
_ _ _ _ _			
white			
_ _ _ _ _			

Match and write it.

whip   think   when   bath   thin

thick   white   math   whale   path

Spell. | | | | Write.

	th	sh	e	i	nk	s
	th	wh	a	i	p	m
	p	m	i	a	ll	th
	d	b	o	a	th	lt
	v	wh	i	e	le	te
	wh	sh	o	a	le	p
	wh	th	i	a	nk	n

Yes or no?

	No	Yes
Can a whale swim?	☐	☐
Will a throne shave?	☐	☐
Can a whip think?	☐	☐
Can a dress be white?	☐	☐
Will a clock take a bath?	☐	☐
Can a path go to my home?	☐	☐
Will a fish grab a whale?	☐	☐

X it.

The pet did math. ☐ The pet had a bath. ☐	
Tim gave me thin socks. ☐ Tim gave me a white box. ☐	
A rake is on the path. ☐ A cake is in the bath. ☐	
The snack is in the whale. ☐ The whale is in the shed. ☐	
Mat is on the slide. ☐ Math is in the sky. ☐	
Sam stuck the whip in the cake. ☐ Sam whips a stick in the lake. ☐	
Pat and Pam share the stove. ☐ Pam pats the snake. ☐	

Write it.

51

ch says /ch/ as in <u>ch</u>air.

X the picture that begins with /ch/.

ch-			
ch-			
ch-			

-tch at the end of a word says /ch/ as in wa<u>tch</u>.

X the picture that ends with /ch/.

-tch			
-tch			
-tch			

	chick chuck catch		chop class chess
	clap chip ship		pitch patch punch
	chin chill shell		lunch bunch land
	bent bank bench		watch witch wick
	crash chair chess		catch chick crutch

Read, write, and X it.

punch			
_ _ _ _ _			
chin			
_ _ _ _			
chop			
_ _ _ _			
inch			
_ _ _ _			
chess			
_ _ _ _ _			
rich			
_ _ _ _			
crutch			
_ _ _ _ _ _			

54

Match and write it.

chess   chop   catch   bench   patch

chip   chin   chick   lunch   chill

	th ch	e	i	ss ll
	ch cl	o	e	t p
	th ch	u	i	ll f
	c s	a	o	th tch
	p r	i	a	sh ch
	d p	a	o	tch ck
	m b	a en		ct ch

Yes or no?

	No	Yes
Can a dish chop a stone?	☐	☐
Will a bench skip?	☐	☐
Can a patch be on a dress?	☐	☐
Can a chick catch a man?	☐	☐
Can you drink punch in a hut?	☐	☐
Can a pet use a crutch?	☐	☐
Will lunch be on a fish?	☐	☐

X it.

Jen has a chill.	☐	
Jen has a chin.	☐	
I will chop the crutch.	☐	
I will hop on a crutch.	☐	
Chaz will fly a kite at the lake.	☐	
The fish will try to catch the frog.	☐	
Chet will crash on the bench.	☐	
Chet can catch the jet.	☐	
Hope has a white plane.	☐	
Hope has a white plate.	☐	
Mitch will try to patch the dish.	☐	
Mitch will try to punch the gate.	☐	
Bet drinks pink punch.	☐	
Bet stands by the bench.	☐	

Write it.

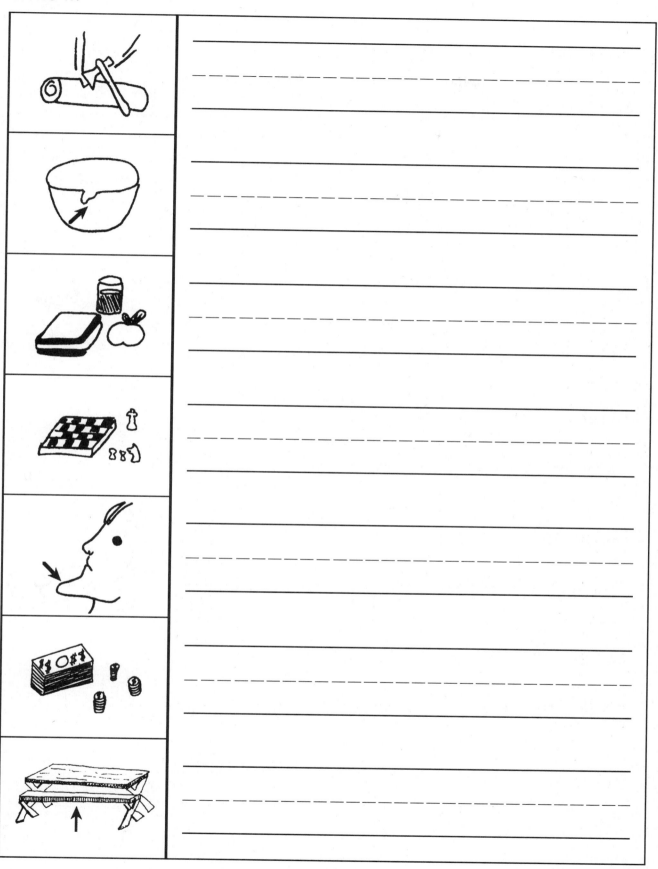

-ng says /ng/ as in ri<u>ng</u>.

X the picture that ends with /ng/.

-ng			
-ng			
-ng			

-ck says /k/ as in clo<u>ck</u>.

X the picture that ends with /k/.

-ck			
-ck			
-ck			

it.

tack track tick	sing ring rind
gag gang rang	wing rang wind
think bring thing	lock log lack
mock neck nest	sick stuck stick
sting king sling	swim sink swing

Read, write, and X it.

king _ _ _ _			
ring _ _ _ _			
sing _ _ _ _			
chick _ _ _ _ _			
tack _ _ _ _			
sick _ _ _ _			
hang _ _ _ _			

Match and write it.

hang	sting	chick	sing	tack
lock	ring	neck	wing	swing

_____

_____

_____

_____

_____

_____

_____

_____

	t r	i	o	ng nt
	st sh	u i	ng m
	b h	a o	n ng
	sm sw	i e	nt ng
	ch th	a i	ss ck
	s st	i e	ck ng
	m n	e a	ss ck

64

Yes or no?

	No	Yes
Can a gang sing?	☐	☐
Will a ring like a snack?	☐	☐
Will a stick take a bath?	☐	☐
Will a chick have a wing?	☐	☐
Can a lock sing to me?	☐	☐
Can I hang a map up with a tack?	☐	☐
Will a swing fit in a sock?	☐	☐

X it.

Ted has a sting.	☐	
Ted can sing.	☐	
A wing is on the king.	☐	
A ring is on the clock.	☐	
The trap hangs on the nest.	☐	
The tag hands on my neck.	☐	
The swing is on the shack.	☐	
The swing is on the snake.	☐	
It takes a long time to fix the lock.	☐	
It will not take long to set the clock.	☐	
A whale can swing on a rope.	☐	
A class can sing on a rock.	☐	
The fat frog has lunch.	☐	
The fast chick can punch.	☐	

Write it.

⬭ it.	shack snake shake
	pack junk joke
	witch mash match
	ding-dong sing-song ping-pong
	sack snack snake
	snare shape shore
	which whine wind
	scare skip store
	chase check case
	rose frame froze

Read and X it.

	check	chess	such
	snack	snatch	snake
	throne	throb	shone
	crash	track	trash
	check	catch	chick
	struck	strong	sting
	branch	such	bench

Read, write, and X it.

whine ------			
shape ------			
snake ------			
tick-tock ------			
shine ------			
white ------			
match ------			

	sh sn	a o	le ke	
	w m	i a	tch sh	
	ch sh	e a	ck ne	
	tr thr	u o	ne ng	
	sh ch	i e	ss st	
	wh th	a i	le te	
	str sh	i o	mp ng	

71

Yes or no?

	No	Yes
Will a stick whine?	☐	☐
Can a witch tell a joke?	☐	☐
Can we drive to the joke shop?	☐	☐
Is a match glad to shave?	☐	☐
Will a fish go tick-tock?	☐	☐
Can I shake a leg?	☐	☐
Will a bench chase a whale?	☐	☐

X it.

A match can smile.	☐	
A mat can doze.	☐	
The cake froze in the cube.	☐	
The cube froze on the skate.	☐	
The pup will smile at lunch.	☐	
The pup swims to lunch.	☐	
A snake sits on the stove.	☐	
The white clock is on sale.	☐	
Jane will try to catch the pet.	☐	
Jane made a sketch of Pete.	☐	
The bike can chase the class.	☐	
The class will chase the kite.	☐	
A fish can tell a cute joke.	☐	
Tish can sell a fine rake.	☐	

Write it.

ee says /ē/ as in tr<u>ee</u>.

$\bigcirc$ it.

feel
heel
feet

deep
deer
been

jeer
peep
jeep

sleep
sheep
sheet

three
thrill
tree

peel
prick
peek

steep
sweep
sweet

cheese
cheer
chess

Read, write, and X it.

tree			
_ _ _ _			
teeth			
_ _ _ _ _			
wheel			
_ _ _ _ _			
queen			
_ _ _ _ _			
cheese			
_ _ _ _ _ _			
feed			
_ _ _ _			
feet			
_ _ _ _			

76

ea says /ē/ as in <u>ear</u>.

( ) it.

leaf	lead leak leaf	drum clean dream

 reap
read
real

bead
beak
deed

 seal
seat
seed

 stem
seam
steam

 track
three
treat

 seat
seem
eats

77

Read, write, and X it.

ear _ _ _			
beak _ _ _ _			
treat _ _ _ _ _			
clean _ _ _ _ _			
speak _ _ _ _ _			
meal _ _ _ _			
steal _ _ _ _ _			

78

Match and write it.

tree	speak	queen	steam	sweep
read	deer	sheep	ear	dream

_____

_____

_____

_____

_____

_____

_____

_____

	br tr	ee at	
	b t	ee e	ch th
	s sw	a ea	l t
	ch cl	ea oa	n m
	f j	ai ee	d t
	l t	e ea	f k
	wh m	a ee	k l

Yes or no?

	No	Yes
Can a jeep fly?	☐	☐
Will a sheep sweep the path?	☐	☐
Will she like a treat?	☐	☐
Will a chick brush its beak?	☐	☐
Can a twig speak?	☐	☐
Can I dream of fun?	☐	☐
Will a queen sit on a leaf?	☐	☐

X it.

The tree has a leaf.	☐	
The tree has a meal.	☐	
Sal has a ship in the jeep.	☐	
Sal has a sheep in the jeep.	☐	
Jim can beat a drum in the street.	☐	
Jim can beat a drum in the tree.	☐	
The queen has a treat on the seat.	☐	
The queen has teeth on the seat.	☐	
Tim can sweep up the dump.	☐	
Tim can sneak up on the deer.	☐	
The king eats with the whale.	☐	
The whale reads with the dog.	☐	
Dave dreams of a big meal.	☐	
Dave cleans up a big mess.	☐	

ai and ay say /ā/ in p<u>ai</u>l and p<u>ay</u>.

Ai is at the beginning or in the middle of a word.
Ay is at the end of a word.

 it.

seal
sail
sat

sail
snail
snore

peel
beam
pail

hay
here
heat

team
track
train

step
stain
stay

meal
nail
name

play
pray
peek

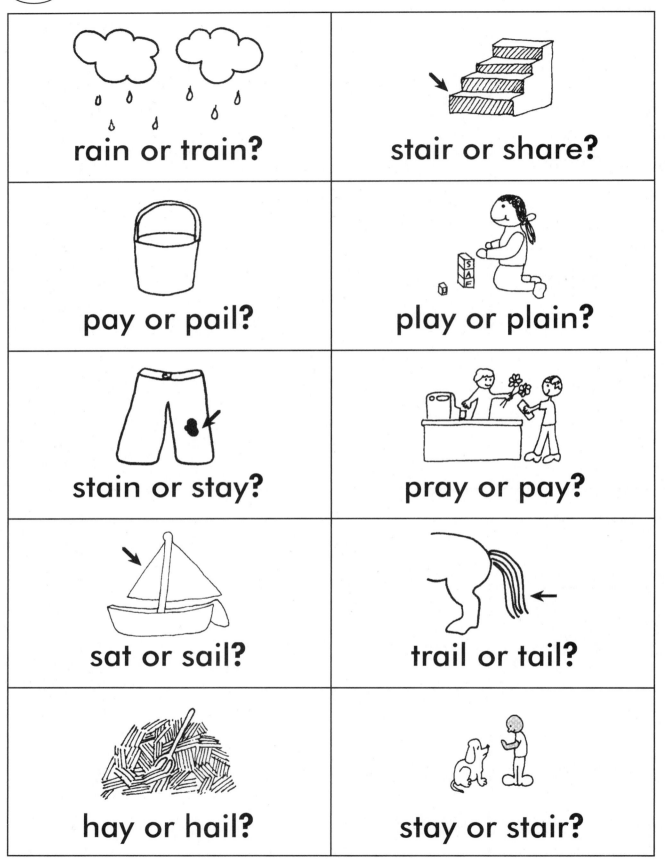

○ it.

rain or train?	**stair or share?**
pay or pail?	**play or plain?**
stain or stay?	**pray or pay?**
sat or sail?	**trail or tail?**
hay or hail?	**stay or stair?**

Read, write, and X it.

stay _ _ _ _			
pail _ _ _ _			
hair _ _ _ _			
tail _ _ _ _			
chain _ _ _ _ _			
stair _ _ _ _ _			
hay _ _ _			

Match and write it.

chain	nail	stay	stain	rain
play	day	hay	pray	pail

	p b	ea ai	l t	_____
	ch th	ee ai	r t	_____
	s n	ea ai	t l	_____
	ch th	ai ee	m n	_____
	h n	ai ay	m r	_____
	r gr	ee ai	u n	_____
	tw tr	ay ai	n m	_____

87

Yes or no?

	No	Yes
Is hay made of hair?	☐	☐
Will a nail play with me?	☐	☐
Can you drive a jeep in the rain?	☐	☐
Will a chain eat on the street?	☐	☐
Do sheep swim on a train?	☐	☐
Can we try to clean a stain?	☐	☐
Is it a treat to stay in jail?	☐	☐

X it.

Rain hits the mail. ☐

Rain hits the meal. ☐

The train stays on the track. ☐

The train stops on the treat. ☐

Glen has his feet on the stove. ☐

Glen has the stairs on his feet. ☐

The sheep hangs its tail in the rain. ☐

The sheet has hay on a plate. ☐

Jean will sell hay at the shack. ☐

Jean will sail in a pail. ☐

The dog plays on its chain. ☐

The dog will stay on the chair. ☐

Steve stays in the rain for a day. ☐

Steve plays on the jeep this way. ☐

Write it.

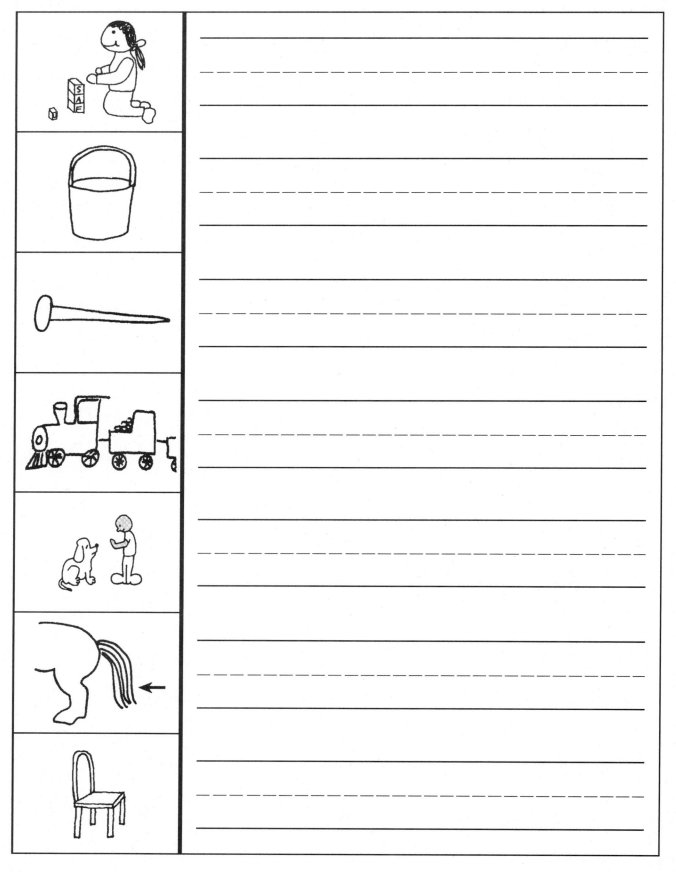

Lesson 12

oa and ow say /ō/ as in b<u>oa</u>t and bl<u>ow</u>.

Oa is at the beginning or in the middle of a word.
Ow is at the end of a word.

 it.

row glow rope	grow goat gait
bow boat blow	read raid road
three throw tow	flat fleet float
show slow snow	coat crow coal

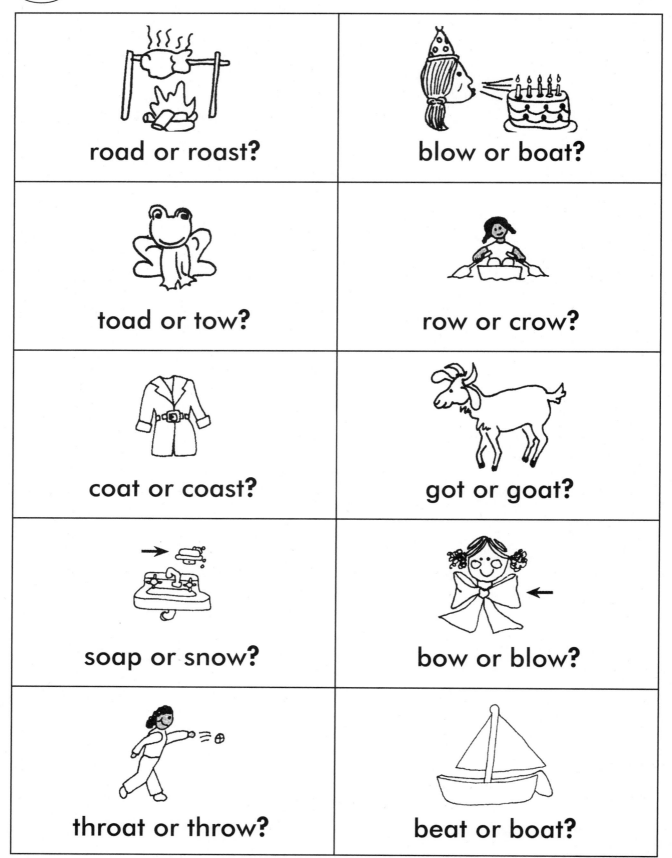

( ) it.

road or roast?	blow or boat?
toad or tow?	row or crow?
coat or coast?	got or goat?
soap or snow?	bow or blow?
throat or throw?	beat or boat?

Read, write, and X it.

snow _ _ _ _			
roast _ _ _ _ _			
blow _ _ _ _			
float _ _ _ _ _			
mow _ _ _			
boat _ _ _ _			
toast _ _ _ _ _			

Match and write it.

snow	goat	boat	throw	mow
coat	blow	soap	slow	toad

	bl dr	oa ow		_____
	s r	ai oa	p d	_____
	t c	oa ea	ze st	_____
	sn sw	ay ow		_____
	th thr	ee ow		_____
	r t	oa ea	p d	_____
	c g	ow oa	t st	_____

Yes or no?

	No	Yes
Can you mow a roast?	☐	☐
Can a toad blow its nose?	☐	☐
Will a coat grow?	☐	☐
Can I row a boat in the rain?	☐	☐
Will a goat go to the show?	☐	☐
Will soap float on a dry road?	☐	☐
Can snow by thick and deep?	☐	☐

X it.

Pat will row the boat. ☐ Pat will throw the boat. ☐	
The toad will fry the meat fast. ☐ The log with the toad floats. ☐	
Pam likes to roast a hot dog. ☐ Pam hates beans on toast. ☐	
We will clean the sails of the boat. ☐ We gave Ned a clean coat. ☐	
The goat eats soap. ☐ The goat is slow to read. ☐	
The chick will mow the grass. ☐ The chick will mop up the glass. ☐	
The snow blows in the road. ☐ The snow blows on the roast. ☐	

Write it.

ee and ea say /ē/.
ai and ay say /ā/.
oa and ow say /ō/.

⬭ it.

sail seal seat	cheat chase cheese
sled sleet sleep	street spree spray
roast reach beach	read braid bride
float fleet flock	three throw treat

it.

wheel or whale?	cheap or clean?
teeth or teach?	row or ray?
roast or reach?	speak or spray?
seal or sail?	paint or pain?
sneak or snail?	feet or float?

Read, write, and X it.

braid _ _ _ _ _			
sleep _ _ _ _ _			
seal _ _ _ _			
eat _ _ _			
spray _ _ _ _ _			
chair _ _ _ _ _			
float _ _ _ _ _			

Match and write it.

wheel	mean	spray	seal	cheese
row	paint	chair	braid	reach

_____

_____

_____

_____

_____

_____

_____

_____

sh s	ea ai	l t	
ch wh	oa ee	t se	
p pl	ai ay	nt t	
f fl	oa ee	n t	
spr sp	ow ay		
sl sh	ee ai	b p	
t r	ea oa	ch t	

Yes or no?

	No	Yes
Can you braid a nail?	☐	☐
Will I use my teeth to eat meat?	☐	☐
Will a train have a wheel?	☐	☐
Can you teach a toad to paint?	☐	☐
Will a seal sweep the road?	☐	☐
Can you roast snow?	☐	☐
Can Fred spray with a hose?	☐	☐

X it.

The goat will fly to the lake.	☐	
The coat will fly to the land.	☐	
The goat has its teeth in the roast.	☐	
The goat has its feet in the road.	☐	
The flakes of snow float by.	☐	
The slow boat rows by.	☐	
Pat can reach the chain.	☐	
Pat can read in the chair.	☐	
Jean sneaks into show and tell.	☐	
Jean shows me the snake.	☐	
Joan dips the brush in the pond.	☐	
The mean brush dips Joan in the paint.	☐	
The toad swings in the rain.	☐	
The toad sings on the train.	☐	

Write it.

Book 3 — Posttest

(Teacher dictated. See Key for Books 1 to 5.)

1. spray spree stay pray	2. share sheer shack shore
3. reach rain raise roast	4. wheat wheel whale waist
5. chain cheat chair coach	6. soak sneak snore snail
7. moan mean meet main	8. flee float flay flow
9. paint pain poach peach	10. toast teach taste teeth

*For further practice, see Book 3½, pp. 113–120.

(Teacher dictated. See Key for Books 1 to 5.)

1. _____

2. _____

3. _____

4. _____

5. _____

6. _____

Read, and then write the word:

1. I put on a mask and say, "Trick or tr_____."

2. I like to coast on my sled in the deep sn_____.

3. When I use the stove, I like to bake a c_____.

4. When you eat a meal, you sit on a ch_____.

5. Please do not pull the dog by its t_____.

6. When I go to sleep, I have a dr_____.

Read, and ⬭ a word:

What Am I?

1. I can grow quite big. I give lots of shade. If you have a rope, you can make a swing in me. I have green leaves. I am a
   > train.
   > tree.
   > tray.

2. I am white. You may not like to brush me, but you must. I help you bite your meat. Take good care of me. I am your
   > teach.
   > team.
   > teeth.

3. At times you will row me. You may put up a sail and glide on the lake. I float well. If you do not swim, do not tip me. I am a
   > bow.
   > boat.
   > boast.